OPTIONS TRADING CRASH COURSE

A Beginners' Guide to Investing and Making Profit with the Best Trading Strategies. The Top Tactics to Know for Beginner and Veteran Options Traders

By

Dave Evans

TABLE OF CONTENT

INTRODUCTION

Options trading can be daunting for those with little to no experience, but it doesn't have to be. Options are a simple tool that allows you to increase your returns on investments and leverage the power of buying low and selling high.

In this article, we'll explore the basics of options trading so that you can start to educate yourself about how they work. We'll talk about what they are, the different types and when you might use them.

What Are Options?

There are many ways to make money in the stock market. You can buy a stock outright, you can short sell stocks and you could even trade options. The first thing you need to understand about options is that they are contracts that give the buyer the right to buy or sell a stock at a specific price before a specific date. Call Options are the right to buy stocks at a predetermined price and Put Options are the right to sell stocks at a predetermined price. There is a buyer and a seller for every option and the seller is obligated to fulfill the contract the buyer should choose to exercise it.

If you're using options as a way to trade stocks, a put option is basically insurance against losing money. If you own stocks and fear they might drop in value, you can buy put option contracts to protect the stocks from losing too much. If the stocks don't drop, you don't have to do anything else and your put option expires worthless. If the stock drops below the strike price, you can sell your stocks at the predetermined price and then buy them back with the option contract. That way you avoid losing money on your original investment. If you're looking to trade options as an investment strategy on its own, then buying call option contracts is a good way to do it. If you think a stock is going to go up in value, you can buy call option contracts with a strike price that's higher than the current market price. That way you can make money if the stock goes up. If the stock doesn't go up, your option expires worthless and you lose the money that you paid for it. Your goal in that situation would be to buy the stocks at the strike price and then sell them for a higher price. Options are a great way to trade stocks or build your investment portfolio.

Types of Options

There are two main types of options: equity and index.

Equity options are the rights to buy a specific stock at a specific price in the future. Index options are rights to buy or sell an entire index, like the S&P

500. You can also trade options on futures contracts, which are

agreements to buy or sell a specific commodity at a specific price in the future.

These are known as futures options but they work in similar ways to equity and index options.

You can also trade options on currency pairs. Instead of buying the US dollar or any other currency, you can buy options on the exchange rate between two currencies. In this case, the underlying asset is currencies and not stocks.

Using Options in Your Portfolio

One of the great things about options trading is that it lets you take a more active role in your portfolio. If you have stocks that are performing poorly but you still think they have the potential to go up, you can buy put option contracts to protect your investment. This way you don't have to sell your stocks and take a loss, giving them a second chance to go up in value. Buying put option contracts is also a great way to hedge your portfolio.

If you have stocks that are doing well but you're afraid that they might have a correction, you can buy put option contracts to protect your portfolio. If the stocks don't drop in value, you don't have to do anything and your put option contracts expire worthlessly. If your stocks do drop in value, the put option contracts allow you to sell your stocks at the predetermined price and then buy them back with the option contract. This way you can avoid losing money on your original investment. You can do it too!

Options trading can seem like a daunting task, but it doesn't have to be. It can be a simple way to trade stocks or the underlying assets of futures contracts. You can start by reading up on the basics of options and learning how they work. This way you can get a better idea of how they can work for you and how to use them. You don't have to dive right into the deep end, especially if you're just starting out. The best way to learn how to swim is to step into the shallow end and slowly wade into the deeper water. This will give you time to get comfortable with the process and then gradually build up your confidence.

Hopefully, by now you have a solid understanding of options trading. You don't have to use them on your own or as part of an active trading strategy. You can use options as a way to build your investment portfolio, protect your investments, and work towards meeting your goals.

You can also use options to trade stocks. Whatever you decide to do with them, having a solid understanding of options trading will help you make the right decision for yourself.

1

OPTIONS TRADING BASICS

Trading options is a great deal like trading stocks, however, there are significant differences. In contrast to stocks, options come in two kinds (puts and calls) and these options are contracts (as opposed to shares) that give the owner the right to purchase or sell fundamental security like a stock. Like stocks, in any case, options are exchanged on trades and individual dealers can get solicitations to buy and sell through a financier firm.

Options trading isn't new. Indeed, the primal listed options contract made its presentation on the Chicago Board Options Exchange in 1973. While an option today is fundamentally the same as what it was around then, numerous things have changed. The greatest distinction is the size of the market in terms of contracts traded, investors, and several trades. It has developed exponentially and there are more individuals trading options now than ever before.

Investors use options for a wide range of reasons. A call option is an agreement that gives the investor the option to purchase a stock at a set cost for a certain timeframe. A few investors purchase calls when they expect the offer cost to move higher. Others may sell calls when they expect that the cost of stock should move lower or trade flat.

A put option represents the right to sell a security at a pre-decided value (the strike cost) for a predefined timeframe. An investor may purchase a put if they expect that the cost of stock should move lower or as a protective position. A put seller is committed to purchasing the stock at the strike cost through a lapse period.

Calls and puts can be utilized in a bunch of approaches to make distinctive potential rewards and risks situations. Complex strategies like butterflies, straddles, and calendars lie outside the extent of this book, however, regardless of the option contract or the motivation for selling and purchasing, the orders are submitted to a brokerage firm and afterward the transaction happen one of the trades.

Before we dig profound into the universe of options trading, let's take a minute to comprehend why we need options at all. If you are thinking it is simply another approach to bring in money and was made by some extravagant folks in suits working in Wall Street, well, you are incorrect. The options world originates before the modern stock trades by an enormous margin.

While some praise the Samurai for giving us the establishment on which options contracts were based, some recognize the Greeks for giving us a thought on the most proficient method to how to speculate on a commodity, for this situation, the harvest of olives. In the two cases, people were attempting to figure the cost of a food thing and trade accordingly, sometime before the advanced world put in various guidelines and set up trades.

Because of this, let us try to address the primary question in your mind.

OPTIONS TRADING GUIDE FOR BEGINNERS

What is options trading?

How about we take a very simple example to comprehend options trading. Consider that you are purchasing a stock for Rs. 3000. However, the broker informs you regarding an energizing offer, that you can get it now for Rs. 3000 or you can give a token of Rs. 30 and reserve the right to purchase it at Rs. 3000 following a month, even if the stock increments in value at that time. But, that amount is non- refundable!

You understand that there is a high possibility that the stock would cross Rs. 3030 and in this way, you can breakeven at least. Since you need to pay just Rs. 30 now, the remaining amount can be utilized somewhere else for a month. You sit tight for a month and afterward take a look at the stock cost.

Presently, contingent upon the stock price, you have the choice to purchase the stock from the broker or not. This is an over- simplification; however, this is options trading in a gist. In the universe of trading, options are instruments that belong to the subsidiary's family, which implies its cost is gotten from something else, generally stocks. The cost of an option is intrinsically connected to the cost of the underlying stock.

Options are contingent subordinate agreements that permit purchasers of the agreements (option holders) to purchase or sell a security at a picked cost. Option purchasers are charged a sum called a "premium" by the sellers for such a right. Should market price be disparaging for option holders, they will let the option expire worthlessly, thus ensuring the losses are not greater than the premium.

Interestingly, option sellers assume more serious risk than the option purchasers, which is the reason they demand this premium.

Options are divided into "put" and "call" options. With a call option, the purchaser of the contract buys the option to purchase the fundamental asset later on at a foreordained price, called strike price or exercise price. With a put option, the purchaser gets the option to sell the fundamental asset in the future at the predetermined price.

Why Trade Options Instead Of a Direct Asset?

The Chicago Board of Options Exchange (CBOE) is the greatest such trade in the world, offering options on a wide range of indexes, ETF's, and single stocks. Traders can develop option strategies ranging from buying or offering a single option to extremely complex ones that include diverse concurrent option positions.

Below are rudimentary option techniques for beginners.

Buying Calls (Long Call)

This is the preferred technique for traders who:

- Are "bullish" or confident on a specific stock, index or ETF and want to confine risk

- Want to use influence to take advantage of rising costs

Options are leveraged instruments, i.e., they permit traders to enhance the advantage by risking littler sums than would somehow be required if trading the underlying asset itself. A standard option contract on a stock controls a hundred shares of fundamental security.

Assume a broker needs to put $5,000 in Apple (AAPL), trading around $165 per share. With this sum, the person in question can buy 30 offers for $4,950. Assume then that the cost of the stock increments by 10% to $181.50 throughout the following month. Ignoring any transaction fees, commission, or brokerage, the dealer's portfolio will increase to $5,445, leaving the dealer with a net return of $495, or 10 percent on the investment.

Assume a call option on the stock with a strike cost of $165 that expires about a month from now costs $550 per contract or $5.50 per share. Given the dealer's investment budget, the individual in question can purchase nine options for an expense of $4,950. Since the option contract controls 100 shares, the dealer is adequately arranging 900 shares. If the stock cost expands 10% to $181.50 at lapse, the option will terminate in the money and be worth $16.50 per share ($181.50-$165 strike), or $14,850 on 900 shares. That is a net dollar return of $9,990, or 200% on the capital contributed, a lot bigger return contrasted with trading the fundamental asset straightforwardly.

Reward/Risk: The broker's potential loss from a long call is restricted to the premium paid. Potential profit is boundless, as the option payoff will increment alongside the fundamental asset cost until lapse, and there is hypothetically no restriction to how high it can go.

Long Put (Buying Put)

This is the favored technique for traders who:

- Are bearish on a specific stock, index or ETF, however, want to face less challenge than with a short-selling procedure

- Want to use leverage to take advantage of falling costs

A put option works the specific inverse way a call option does, with the put option picking up an incentive as the cost of the basic reductions. While short-selling additionally permits a broker to profit from falling costs, the risk with a short position is boundless, as there is hypothetically no restriction on how high a cost can rise. With a put option, if the basic increments past the option's strike value, the option will simply expire worthlessly.

Risk/Reward: Possible loss is limited to the premium paid for the options.

The maximum profit from the position is topped since the basic cost can't drop below zero, however, similarly as with a long call option, the put option uses the dealer's return.

Covered Call

This is the favored position for traders who:

- Expect slight increase or no change in the underlying's cost

- Are willing to constrain upside potential in return for some downside protection

A covered call strategy involves purchasing 100 shares of the underlying resource and selling a call option against those shares. At the point when the broker sells the call, he gathers the option's premium, along these lines bringing down the cost premise on the offers and giving some downside protection. Consequently, by selling the option, the broker is consenting to sell shares of the underlying at the option's strike cost, in this manner topping the dealer's upside potential.

Suppose a dealer buys 1,000 shares of (BP) at 44USD per share and at the same time writes 10 call options (1 agreement/contract for every 100 offers) with a strike cost of 46USD expiring in 1 month, to a detriment of 0.25USD per share, or 25USD per contract and 250USD total for the 10 agreements/contract. The 0.25USD premium reduces the price premise on the shares to 43.75USD, so any drop in the underlying down to this point will be balanced by the premium gotten from the option position, along these lines offering restricted downside protection.

If the share value transcends $46 before the lapse, the short call option will be exercised (or "summoned"), which means the trader should deliver the stock at the option's strike cost. For this situation, the broker will make a profit of $2.25 per share ($46 strike cost - $43.75 cost premise).

In any case, this model infers the broker doesn't expect BP to move above $46 or fundamentally beneath $44 throughout the following month. As long as the shares don't rise above $46 and get summoned before the options terminate, the dealer will keep the premium clear and free and can keep selling calls against the shares if he chooses.

Reward/Risk: If the share price transcends the strike cost before the lapse, the short call option can be practiced and the dealer should deliver shares of underling at the option's strike price, even if it is beneath the market price. As a byproduct of this risk, a covered call strategy gives confined drawback protection as premium got when selling the call option.

Protective Put

This is the favored strategy for traders who:

- Own the basic asset and need drawback protection.

A Protective put is a long put, similar to the strategy we talked about above; however, the objective, as the name suggests, is downside protection as opposed to trying to profit from a downside move. If a broker owns shares that the person is bullish on over the long haul but wants to protect against a decrease in the short run, they may buy a protective put.

If the price of the basic increments and is over the put's strike price at development, the option lapses worthless and the dealer loses the premium but at the same time has the benefit of the increased basic price. Then again, if the underlying price diminishes, the trader's portfolio position loses value, however, this loss is to a great extent covered by the gain from the put option position. Subsequently, the position can adequately be thought of as a protection technique.

The broker can set the strike price underneath the present price to lessen premium payment to the detriment of diminishing downside protection. This can be thought of as deductible protection. Assume, for instance, that an investor purchases 1,000 shares of Coca-Cola (KO) for $44 and needs to protect the investment from unfavorable price developments throughout the next two months.

Reward/Risk: If the cost of the basic remains the equivalent or rises, the potential misfortune will be constrained to the option premium, which is paid as protection. If the cost of the underlying falls, the loss in the capital will be balanced by an expansion in the option's cost and is restricted to the distinction between the underlying strike price and stock price in addition to the premium paid for the option. In the above model, at the strike price of 4USD0, the loss is limited to 4.20USD per share (44USD – 40USD + 0.20USD).

Other Options Strategies

These strategies might be somewhat more perplexing than basically purchasing puts or calls, yet they are intended to assist you with bettering deal with the risk of options trading:

- **Buy-write strategy or Covered call strategy:** Stocks are purchased, and the financial specialist sells call options on the same stock. The number of shares you purchased ought to be identical to the number of call options contracts you sold.

- **Married Put Strategy:** After buying a stock, the dealer buys put options for an equivalent number of shares. The married put works like an insurance approach against momentary losses call options with a specific strike price. At the same time, you will sell the same number of call options at a higher strike cost.

- **Protective Collar Strategy:** A dealer buys an out-of-the- money put option, while all the while working an out-of-the- money call option for a comparable stock.

- **Long Straddle Strategy:** The dealer buys a put option and a call option simultaneously. The two options ought to have the same strike price and the same expiration.

- **Long Strangle Strategy:** Investor buys an out-of-the-money put option and a call option simultaneously. They have a similar lapse date, but, they have differing strike prices. The put strike price should be lower than the call strike price.

Options offer alternative techniques for investors to profit from trading protections. There's an assortment of strategies involving underlying assets, various combinations of options, and other derivatives. Fundamental methodologies for beginners incorporate purchasing calls, purchasing puts, selling covered calls, and purchasing protective puts. There are advantages to trading options as opposed to underlying assets, for example, leveraged returns and downside protection, but there are also disadvantages like the necessity for forthright premium payment. Picking a broker is the first step to trading options.

A formal definition is given below:

A stock option is an agreement between two people or parties wherein the stock option purchaser (holder) buys the right (but not the responsibility) to purchase/sell shares of a basic stock at a fixed price from/to the option seller (writer) within a given period.

OPTIONS TRADING VS. STOCK TRADING

There must be uncertainty in your mind that why do we have options trading if it is simply another method of trading. Indeed, here are a couple of points which make it unique to trading stocks;

- The Options contract has a lapse date, unlike stocks. The termination can vary from weeks, months to years contingent on the guidelines and the sort of Options that you are practicing. Stocks, on the other hand, don't have a termination or expiration date.

- Unlike Stocks, Options get their value from something different and that is the reason they fall under the derivatives class.

- Options are not distinct by numbers like Stocks.

- Options proprietors/owners have no right (dividend or voting) in an organization, unlike Stock owners.

Some people often find the Option's concept hard to comprehend, however, they have just tailed it in their other transactions, for example, mortgages or car insurance.

OPTIONS TERMINOLOGIES

Premium

Since the Options themselves do not have fundamental value, the Options premium is the price that you need to pay to buy an Option. The premium is dictated by different variables including the underlying stock value, unpredictability in the market, and the days until the Option's expiration. In options trading, picking the premium is one of the most significant components.

Strike Price

This is the price at which the underlying stocks can be sold or purchased according to the agreement/contract. In options trading, the Strike Price for a Call Option shows the cost at which the Stock can be purchased (on or before its termination date) and for Put Options trading it alludes to the cost at which the seller can practice its entitlement to sell the underlying stocks (on or before its termination)

Underlying Asset

In options trading, the fundamental asset can be stocks, index, commodity, futures, or currency. The price of Options is gotten from its underlying asset. The Option of stock gives the option to purchase or sell the stock at a particular cost and date to the holder. Thus, it is all about the fundamental stocks or assets when it comes to Stock in

Options Trading.

Expiration Date

In options trading, every single stock option has an expiration date. The expiration date is the last date on which the Options holder can practice the right to purchase or sell the Options that are in holding. In Options Trading, the expiration of Options can vary from weeks to months to years contingent upon the regulations and the market.

Options Style

There are two significant sorts of Options that are practiced in most of the options trading markets.

- American Options which can be practiced anytime before its lapse date

- European Options must be practiced upon the arrival of its lapse or expiration.

Moneyness (ITM, OTM & ATM)

It is imperative to comprehend the Options Moneyness before you begin trading in Stock Options. A great deal of options trading methodologies is played around the Moneyness of an Option.

It essentially defines the connection between the strike cost of an Option and the present cost of the underlying Stocks. We will look at each term in detail below.

When is an Option in-the-money?

- Put Option - when the underlying strike price is higher than the stock price.

- Call Option – when the underlying strike price is lower than the stock price.

When is an Option out-of-the-money?

- Call Option – when the underlying strike price is higher than the stock price.

- Put Option – this is when the underlying strike price is lower than the stock price.

When is an Option at-the-money?

- When the underlying stock cost is equivalent to the strike cost

- Take a break here to consider over the various terms as we will discover it incredibly helpful later when we go through the kinds of options just as a couple of options trading techniques.

TYPE OF OPTIONS

In a genuine sense, there are just two types of Options i.e Put and Call Options. We will understand them in more detail.

To Call or Put

A Call Option is an option to purchase an underlying Stock on or before its termination date. At the hour of purchasing a Call Option, you pay a specific amount of premium to the seller which awards you the right (but not the responsibility) to purchase the underlying stock at a predetermined value (strike price).

Buying a call option implies that you are bullish about the market and trusting that the cost of the underlying stock may go up. To make a profit, the cost of the stock ought to go higher than the strike cost plus the premium of the call option that you have bought before or at the hour of its lapse.

Excitingly, a Put Option is an option to sell an underlying Stock on or before its termination date. Buying a Put Option implies that you are bearish about the market and trusting that the cost of the underlying stock may go down. With the end goal for you to make a profit, the cost of the stock ought to go down from the strike price in addition to the premium of the Put Option that you have bought previously or at the hour of its termination.

Thusly, both Call and Put option purchaser's loss is constrained to the premium paid, however, profit is boundless. The above clarifications were from the purchaser's perspective. We will now comprehend the put-call options from the seller's perspective, which is options writers. The Put option sellers, as an end-result of the premium charged, are committed to purchasing the basic asset at the strike price. In like manner, the Call option seller, as a final product of the premium charged, is focused on selling the fundamental asset at the strike price.

Is there an approach to envision the potential profit/loss of an option purchaser or seller? In reality, there is. An option payoff is a graphical portrayal of the Net Profit/Loss made by the option purchasers and sellers.

Before we go through the charts, how about we comprehend what the four terms mean. As we realize that going short means selling and going long means purchasing the asset, a similar rule applies to options.

- Short call - Here we bet that the costs will fall and henceforth, a short call implies you are selling calls.

- Short put - Here the short put implies we are selling a put option.

- Long put - Here we are purchasing a put option.

- Long call - it implies that we are purchasing a call option since we are hopeful about the underlying asset's share cost.

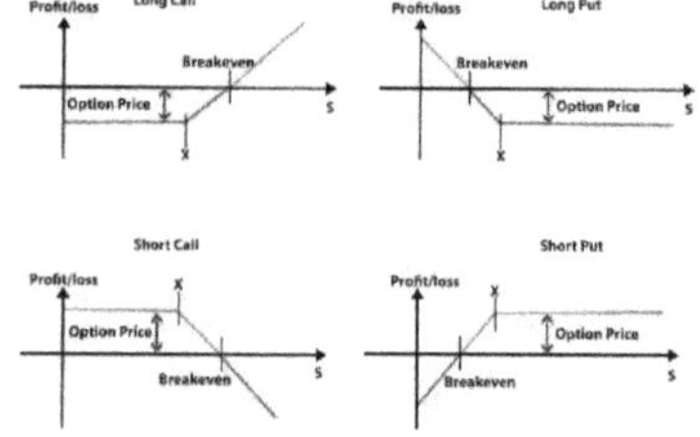

where

S = Underlying Price X = Strike Price

The breakeven point is that point where you make no loss or no profit.

The long call holder makes a profit equivalent to the stock cost at termination less strike price less premium if the option is in the money. Call option holder makes a loss equivalent to the amount of premium if the option lapses out of money and the writer of the option makes a flat profit equivalent to the option premium.

So also, for the put option purchaser, profit is made when the option is in the money and is equivalent to the strike value less the stock cost at lapse less premium. Also, the put writer makes a profit equivalent to the premium for the option.

OK, until now we have been going through a ton of hypotheses. We should shift gears for a moment and come to reality. What do options look like? All things considered, let's find out.

What does an options trading quote comprise of?

If you somehow managed to search for an option quote on Apple stock, it would look something like this:

When this was recorded, the stock price of Apple Inc. was $196. Now let's take one line from the list and break it down further.

Eg.

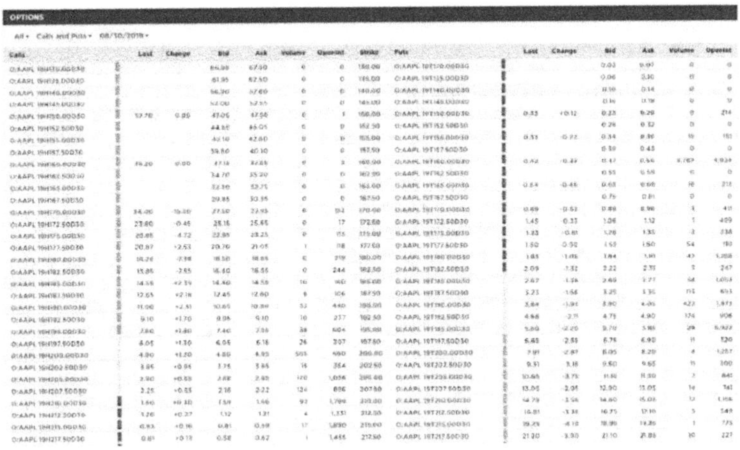

Calls	Last	Change	Bid	Ask	Volume	Openint	Strike	Puts	Last	Change	Bid	Ask	Volume	Openint
O:AAPL 19H135.00D30			66.95	67.50	0	0	135.00	O:AAPL 19T135.00D30			0.03	0.07	0	0
O:AAPL 19H135.00D30			61.95	62.50	0	0	135.00	O:AAPL 19T135.00D30			0.06	0.10	0	0
O:AAPL 19H140.00D30			56.30	57.00	0	0	140.00	O:AAPL 19T140.00D30			0.10	0.14	0	0
O:AAPL 19H145.00D30			52.00	52.55	0	0	145.00	O:AAPL 19T145.00D30			0.16	0.18	0	0
O:AAPL 19H150.00D30	52.70	0.00	47.05	47.50	0	1	150.00	O:AAPL 19T150.00D30	0.33	+0.12	0.23	0.29	0	274
O:AAPL 19H152.50D30			44.55	45.05	0	0	152.50	O:AAPL 19T152.50D30			0.26	0.52	0	0
O:AAPL 19H155.00D30			42.10	42.60	0	0	155.00	O:AAPL 19T155.00D30	0.31	-0.72	0.34	0.39	10	151
O:AAPL 19H157.50D30			39.80	40.10	0	0	157.50	O:AAPL 19T157.50D30			0.39	0.43	0	0
O:AAPL 19H160.00D30	44.20	0.00	37.15	37.85	0	3	160.00	O:AAPL 19T160.00D30	0.42	-0.47	0.47	0.56	5,767	4,934
O:AAPL 19H162.50D30			34.70	35.20	0	0	162.50	O:AAPL 19T162.50D30			0.51	0.58	10	0
O:AAPL 19H165.00D30			32.30	32.75	0	0	165.00	O:AAPL 19T165.00D30	0.54	-0.46	0.63	0.66	10	212
O:AAPL 19H167.50D30			29.85	30.35	0	0	167.50	O:AAPL 19T167.50D30			0.75	0.81	0	0
O:AAPL 19H170.00D30	34.00	0.00	27.50	22.95	0	94	170.00	O:AAPL 19T170.00D30	0.89	-0.53	0.88	0.98	1	411
O:AAPL 19H172.50D30	23.60	-0.45	25.15	25.65	0	17	172.50	O:AAPL 19T172.50D30	1.45	0.33	1.04	1.12	1	409
O:AAPL 19H175.00D30	20.45	-4.72	22.95	23.25	0	115	175.00	O:AAPL 19T175.00D30	1.23	-0.81	1.29	1.35	2	338
O:AAPL 19H177.50D30	20.87	-2.53	20.70	21.05	1	118	177.50	O:AAPL 19T177.50D30	1.50	0.50	1.53	1.60	54	180
O:AAPL 19H180.00D30	18.26	-2.95	18.50	18.85	0	319	180.00	O:AAPL 19T180.00D30	1.85	-1.06	1.84	1.91	43	1,058
O:AAPL 19H182.50D30	18.05	-2.55	16.40	16.55	0	244	182.50	O:AAPL 19T182.50D30	2.09	-1.52	2.22	2.35	7	247
O:AAPL 19H185.00D30	14.55	+2.19	14.40	14.55	10	140	185.00	O:AAPL 19T185.00D30	2.67	-1.56	2.46	2.77	64	1,054
O:AAPL 19H187.50D30	12.65	+2.16	12.45	12.60	9	106	187.50	O:AAPL 19T187.50D30	5.25	-1.56	3.25	3.35	115	401
O:AAPL 19H190.00D30	11.00	+2.51	10.65	10.80	53	440	190.00	O:AAPL 19T190.00D30	3.84	-1.91	3.90	4.05	422	3,073
O:AAPL 19H192.50D30	9.10	+1.70	8.95	9.10	10	237	192.50	O:AAPL 19T192.50D30	4.66	-2.11	4.75	4.90	174	906
O:AAPL 19H195.00D30	7.80	+1.80	7.40	7.55	38	404	195.00	O:AAPL 19T195.00D30	5.80	-2.20	5.70	5.85	29	6,027
O:AAPL 19H197.50D30	6.05	+1.30	6.05	6.15	26	307	197.50	O:AAPL 19T197.50D30	6.61	-2.55	6.75	6.90	11	120
O:AAPL 19H200.00D30	4.90	+1.10	4.80	4.95	503	490	200.00	O:AAPL 19T200.00D30	7.91	-2.87	8.05	8.20	4	1,287
O:AAPL 19H202.50D30	3.85	+0.95	3.75	3.85	15	354	202.50	O:AAPL 19T202.50D30	9.51	3.18	9.50	9.65	15	300
O:AAPL 19H205.00D30	2.90	+0.55	2.82	2.92	120	1,056	205.00	O:AAPL 19T205.00D30	10.65	-3.75	11.10	11.30	7	440
O:AAPL 19H207.50D30	2.25	+0.35	2.15	2.22	124	895	207.50	O:AAPL 19T207.50D30	13.05	-2.05	12.90	13.05	14	741
O:AAPL 19H210.00D30	1.60	+0.10	1.59	1.46	97	1,709	210.00	O:AAPL 19T210.00D30	14.75	-3.56	14.90	15.05	13	1,106
O:AAPL 19H212.50D30	1.20	+0.27	1.12	1.31	4	1,333	212.50	O:AAPL 19T212.50D30	16.81	-3.38	16.75	17.10	5	549
O:AAPL 19H215.00D30	0.83	+0.16	0.81	0.99	17	5,890	215.00	O:AAPL 19T215.00D30	19.25	-4.10	18.99	19.25	1	775
O:AAPL 19H217.50D30	0.85	+0.13	0.58	0.67	1	1,455	217.50	O:AAPL 19T217.50D30	21.20	-3.30	21.10	21.85	10	227

Calls	Last	Change	Bid	Ask	Volume	OpenInt	Strike	Puts	Last	Change	Bid	Ask	Volume	OpenInt
O:AAPL 19H170.00D30	34.00	-15.50	27.50	27.95	0	153	170.00	O:AAPL 19T170.00D30	0.89	-0.53	0.89	0.96	3	411

In a typical options chain, you will have a rundown of put and call options with various strike prices and corresponding premiums. The put options details are on the right and the call option details are on the left with the strike price in the middle.

- The option number and the symbol is the first column.

- The "last" column connotes the sum at which the last time the option was purchased.

- "Change" shows the fluctuation between the last two trades of the said options.

- "Bid" column designates the offer submitted for the option. "Ask" shows the asking cost sought by the option seller. "Volume" shows the number of options traded. Here the volume is 0.

- "Open Interest" shows the number of options that can be purchased at that strike price.

The columns are the equivalent for the put options also. Sometimes, the data provider means whether the option is in the money, at the money or out of money too. We need a guide to truly help our comprehension of options trading. Hence, we should go through one at this point.

Options Trading Example

We will go through 2 cases to better comprehend the put and call options.

For the good of simplicity, let us assume the following:

- Cost of Stock when the options are written: $100

- Premium: $5

- Expiration date: one month after the option is purchased

Case one:

The present strike price: $120. Price of stock: $110.

Type of Option	Owner	Moneyness	Result
Call	Options buyer	Out of the money	If the options buyer proceeds to buy the stock from the options seller, the total amount given by the buyer of a stock is: ($120 +$5 = $125) Since it is better to buy the stock directly, the buyer would not exercise the option.
Call	Options writer	Out of the money	Since the options buyer does not exercise the option, the options writer makes a profit which is equal to the premium.
Put	Option buyer	In the money	Since the options buyer can sell the stock at $120 and thus, the total amount gained in the process ($120 - $5) = $115, which is higher than the stock at $110, the options buyer will exercise the put option.
Put	Option writer	In the money	As the put option is exercised, The options writer reports a loss of ($120 - $110 - $5) = $5

Case two:

The current strike price: $110. Price of stock: $120.

Since we have gone through the detailed situation of every option, we should join a couple of options together. Let's comprehend a significant concept which numerous experts use in options trading.

Type of Option	Owner	Moneyness	Result
Call	[illegible]	In the money	[illegible]
Call	[illegible]	In the money	[illegible]
Put	Option buyer	Out of the money	[illegible]
Put	Option writer	Out of the money	[illegible]

What is Put-Call Parity In Python?

Put-call parity is an idea that any individual who is keen on options trading needs to comprehend. By gaining a comprehension of put-call parity you can comprehend how the estimation of a call option, put option and the stock are connected. This empowers you to make other synthetic position utilizing different option and stock mix.

The principle of put-call parity

The rule of Put-call parity describes the association between the cost of a European Call option and European Put option, both having the equal expiration date, strike price, and underlying asset. If there is a deviation from put-call parity, at that point it would result in an exchange opportunity. Traders would make the most of this chance to make riskless profits till the time the put-call equality is set up once more.

The put-call parity rule can be utilized to approve an option estimating model. If the option costs as computed by the model disregard the put-call parity rule, such a model can be viewed as incorrect.

Understanding Put-Call Parity

To comprehend put-call parity, consider a portfolio "A" encompassing call option and money. The amount of money held equals the call strike cost. Consider another portfolio "B" including a put option and the underlying asset.

Required Conditions For Put-call Parity

For put-call parity to hold, the accompanying conditions ought to be met. In any case, in reality, they barely remain true and the put-call parity equation may require a few alterations in like manner.

- The underlying stock does not deliver any dividend during the life of the European options

- There are no tax duties There are no exchange costs

- Shorting is permitted and there are no borrow charges

Consequently, put-call parity will hold in a frictionless market with the underlying stock delivering no dividends.

Arbitrage Opportunity

In options trading, when the put-call parity rule gets disregarded, traders will attempt to make the most of the arbitrage opportunity. An arbitrage trader will go long on the disparaged portfolio and short the overstated portfolio to make a risk free profit.

The most effective method to make the most of arbitrage opportunity Let us consider a model with certain numbers to perceive how trade can make the most of arbitrage opportunities. How about we assume that the spot cost of a stock is $31, the risk-free interest rate is 10% yearly, the premium on 3-month European put and call are $2.25 and $3 respectively and the exercise cost is $30.

For this situation, the value of portfolio A will be,

$$C+Xe\text{-}rT = 3+30e\text{-}0.1 * 3/12 = \$32.26$$

The value of portfolio B will be,

$$P + S0 = 2.25 + 31 = \$33.25$$

Portfolio B is exaggerated and consequently, an arbitrageur can earn by going short on portfolio B and long on the portfolio. The accompanying steps can be followed to earn arbitrage profits.

- Short the stock. This will produce a cash inflow of $31.

- Short the put option. This will produce a cash inflow of $2.25. Purchase the call option. This will produce a cash outflow of $3.

- Total cash inflow is - 3 + 2.25 + 31 = $30.25.

- Invest $30.25 in a zero-coupon bond with three months of development with a yield of 10% yearly.

Come back from the zero-coupon bond following 3 months will be 30.25e 0.1 * 3/12 = $31.02.

If the stock price at maturity is over 30USD, the call option will be practiced and if the stock price is lesser than 30USD, the put option will be practiced. In the two circumstances, the arbitrageur will buy one stock at 30USD.

This stock will be utilized to cover the short.

Total profit from the arbitrage = $31.02 - $30 = $1.02

Why is Options Trading alluring?

Options are alluring instruments to trade as a result of the higher yields. An option gives the privilege to the holder to accomplish something, with the 'option' of not to practice that right. Along these lines, the holder can confine his losses and increase his profits.

While the facts show that one option contract is for hundred shares, it is accordingly less risky to pay the premium and not risk the aggregate sum which would need to be utilized if we had purchased the shares instead. In this way, your risk exposure is greatly reduced. However, as a general rule, options trading is unpredictable and that is because options pricing models are very complex and mathematical.

So, how do you evaluate if the option is extremely worth purchasing?

The key to effective options trading strategies includes understanding and executing options pricing models. In this segment, we will get a short comprehension of Greeks in options that will help in making and understanding the pricing models.

OPTIONS PRICING

Options Pricing depends on two sorts of values Intrinsic Value of an option

Remember the moneyness concept that went through a couple of segments back. When the call option stock price is over the strike price or when put option stock price is less than the strike value, the option is said to be "In-The-Money (ITM)", that is, it has an inherent value. Then again, "Out of the money (OTM)" options have no intrinsic value. For "Out Of The Money" OTM call options, the stock price is less than the strike price and for OTM put options; stock price is over the strike price. The price of these options comprises completely of time value.

Time Value of an option

If you take away the amount of intrinsic value from the value of an option, you are left with the time value. It depends on the expiration time. We realize what is characteristic and the time estimation of an option. How do we realize that one option is better than the other, and how to quantify the adjustments in option pricing. How about we take the help of the greeks at this point.

Options Greeks

Greeks are the risk measures related to different situations in options trading. The basic ones are gamma, delta, vega, and theta. With the adjustment in volatility or prices of the basic stock, you have to know how your options pricing would be influenced. Greeks in options assist us with understanding how the different factors, for example, time to expiry, prices, volatility affect the options pricing.

Delta measures the affectability of an option's price to an adjustment in the price of the basic stock. Delta is that options greek which reveals to you how much money a stock option will drop or rise in worth with a $1 drop or rise in the underlying stock. Delta is reliant on basic price, volatility, and time to expiry. While the equation for figuring delta is based on the Black-Scholes option-pricing model, we can write it as,

Delta = [Expected change in Premium] / [Change in the price of the underlying stock] Python Library - Mibian

What is Mibian?

Mibian is an options pricing/estimating Python library executing the Black-Scholes alongside a couple different models for European options on stocks and currencies. We are going to take a look at the Black-Scholes part of this library. Mibian is good with python 2.7 and This library requires scipy to work appropriately.

How to utilize Mibian for BS Model?

The function which constructs the Black-Scholes model in this library is the BS() function. Below is the syntax for this function;

BS ([underlyingPrice, strikePrice, interestRate, daysToExpiration], volatility=x, callPrice=y, putPrice=z)

The primary input is a rundown containing the price, interest rate, strike price, and days to expiration. This rundown must be indicated each time the function is being called. Next, we input the volatility, on the off chance that we are keen on processing the price of the option greeks and options. The BS function will just contain two contentions.

If we are keen on computing the implied volatility, we won't input the volatility, but rather will enter either the put price or the call price. If we are keen on figuring the put-call parity, we will enter both the call price and put price after the rundown. The value returned would be: (call price + price of the bond worth the strike price at maturity) - (put price + underlying asset price)

Derman Kani Model

The Derman Kani model was created to beat the long-standing issue with the Black Scholes model, which is the volatility grin. One of the fundamental assumptions of the Black Scholes model is that the underlying follows an arbitrary walk with steady volatility. Notwithstanding, on ascertaining the inferred volatility for various strikes, it is seen that the volatility curve is certainly not a constant straight line as we would expect, but rather has the state of a smile. The curve of implied volatility against the strike price is known as the volatility smile.

If the Black Scholes model is right, it would imply that the underlying follows a lognormal dispersion and the inferred volatility curve would have been level, but a volatility smile shows that traders are certainly attributing an exceptional non-lognormal distribution to the underlying. This non-lognormal dispersion can be credited to the underlying following a modified random walk, as in the volatility isn't consistent and changes with both stock time and price. To accurately value the options, we would need to know the specific type of the modified random walk.

The Derman Kani model tells the best way to take the inferred volatilities as contributions to deduce the type of the underlying's random walk.

More precisely a unique binomial tree is separated from the smile comparing to the random walk of the underlying, this tree is known as the implied tree. This tree can be utilized to esteem different subsidiaries whose costs are not promptly accessible from the market - for instance, it tends to be utilized in standard, but American options, exotic options, and illiquid European options.

What is the Heston model?

Steven Heston provided a closed organized solution for the price of a European call option on an asset with stochastic volatility. This model was additionally developed to consider the volatility smile, which couldn't be clarified utilizing the Black Scholes model.

The fundamental supposition of the Heston model is that volatility is an arbitrary variable. Hence there are two arbitrary factors, one for the volatility and the other for underlying. For the most part, when the variance of the underlying has been made stochastic, closed structured solutions will not exist anymore.

In any case, this is a significant advantage of the Heston model, that shut structure arrangements do exist for European plain vanilla options. This component additionally makes adjustments to the model feasible.

Brokers, Brokerages, and Floor Brokers

Once you're ready to start trading, you're going to need to find someone to handle your transactions for you. This person or company is known as a broker, and there are several different types.

A "broker" is someone who acts as the middleman (woman) who handles buying and selling assets between investors. Brokers fall into two categories: full commission brokers and discount brokers. Here's a breakdown of each:

- **Full Commission Broker:** this is the traditional broker. They provide advice, handle paperwork, manage accounts (even buying and selling at their discretion depending on the broker/client relationship), and charge the "full" commission rate, which will vary depending on the size of your account.

- **Discount Broker:** these brokers discount their services and count on large numbers of clients to succeed. A discount broker won't offer specific advice (they may publish a newsletter or investment guide sent to all their clients), handle paperwork, or manage your account for you. This is fine for many of today's investors, who want to take charge of their investments rather than rely on a broker. Options traders usually prefer discount brokers to help keep their costs down. Traders do need to do their research before selecting a broker since extra fees can eat into your resources.

- **Brokerage:** a "brokerage" of "brokerage house" is simply a collection of brokers who are part of a company designed for investment management.

Options Types

There are two basic approaches to how options are created and managed. These are known as "American Style Options" and "European Style Options." While there are similarities between the two types, which is important here, it's what they do differently.

While you may think that they use European style in Europe and American style in the United States, that isn't the case. Instead, it varies from investment option to investment option.

Perhaps the most significant difference between the two is those holders of the American style can execute their options at any time before the expiration date. Holders of the European style option do not. Obviously, this can be a big deal depending on the volatility of the investment.

Another difference is the two options styles expire on different days of the week. American style typically expires on the third Friday of the month the contract ends. European style options expire the third Thursday of the month the contract ends.

Generally, stocks and ETFs (Exchange Traded Funds, a type of open-ended fund that can be traded just like stocks) trade under the American style. With stock indices, most trade under the European option style (limited indices such as the S&P 100 are an exception).

Binary Options

These are a special type of option with only a put or call choice. They are very simple propositions of the "yes/no" variety. An example would be a binary option for the price of a stock being greater than $100 share by

4 p.m. You will have a choice of a bid or ask price, which is set by traders based on the perceived likelihood of one being more likely to win.

Binary options bid/ask prices will always be between $100 and $0. If traders feel the likelihood of one side or the other is close, you'll likely see a bid/ask of around $49/$51. If there's a great likelihood of the stock exceeding the target price by the deadline, then the bid/ask might be closer to $85/$87 or higher.

Let's say you paid $51 for your binary option, and the stock makes good. You'll receive the $100 value of the binary option. This gives you a profit of $49 minus commission or fees. You are "in the money." If the stock fails to beat the target price, then you're out the $51 plus commission or fees. You are "out of the money."

The bid and ask price will fluctuate depending on the stock price's movement before the deadline. Because they are very simple, binary options are popular choices for beginning investors and those without a lot of time to spend managing their money. You can purchase more than one binary option contract increasing your profit or loss potential.

Settlement Price Determination

Another difference between the two options styles is how and when the option settlement price is determined. The settlement price for American- style options is determined by the regular closing price of the asset at the end of the trading day, the third Friday of the month. Trades that occur after hours do not have any effect on this price. With European-style options, the settlement price usually isn't known until sometime during the next trading day.

Other Terms

- **"Automatic" Exercise:** your broker will exercise the expiring option to protect you.

- **Auto Trading:** you can make an agreement with your broker to automatically execute a position if certain market conditions are met.

- **Open/Close:** the beginning and end of the trading day. Also used to refer to a security's price at either point. For example: "Shares of ABC Corporation opened higher this morning (or closed lower this afternoon)."

- **Correction:** a stock price drop that quickly rebounds

- **Decay/Time Decay:** it refers to the gradual reduction in the time left for the options contract.

- **Dividend:** companies reward stockholders in one of two ways. The price of the stock can increase, or the company can share profits with shareholders by paying them some of those profits per share held by each stockholder. These payments are called dividends. Generally, the price of the stock declines by an amount similar to the dividend since the company is worthless after paying out that money. If you hold an option for a stock that pays out a dividend during the contract period, the value of that dividend has to be factored into the stock price.

- **Fundamentals:** some investors base their investment decisions on readily available information on a company's finances, assets, and other historical data. These include share price versus historical share price, price to earnings ratio [P/E], cash flow, return on assets, etc.

- **Technical Analysis:** these investors rely on analyzing the behavior of a stock or stocks and look for indicators they feel predict movement.

Technical Analysis Vs. Fundamental Analysis

What Is Technical Analysis?

If you want to fully understand and predict what the entry and exit points in the market should be, then understanding technical analysis should be your first and foremost priority. Fundamental analysis is all about making decisions based on industry trends, valuation, and revenue. On the other hand, technical analysis is about volume and price from historical data. In this method, investors implement behavioral economics and statistical analysis so that they can bridge the gap between market price and intrinsic value.

In technical analysis, there are two different approaches, and it is important that you choose the right one for yourself.

- **Top-Down:** This approach is more about macroeconomic analysis. This means that this approach is less about individual securities and more about the overall economy. The primary focus will be on the economy, and then the focus will shift to the various sectors and then finally to the companies present in those sectors.

- **Bottom-Up:** The next one is just the opposite, where the investors focus more on individual stocks rather than a macroeconomic analysis. If a particular stock seems interesting, then this approach will help in finding the possible entry and exit points in that stock.

What Is Fundamental Analysis?

Now, let us move on to one of the cornerstones of the finance world, that is, fundamental analysis. If you want to predict the future price of underlying securities, then understanding fundamental analysis is very important. There are several components that are studied here to perform an in-depth analysis of the market and understand not only the economy but also the company and the industry in which it operates. Once you have this data in your hands, you will be able to predict the future of market developments and also know what value does the stock of a particular company has. You will also be able to find out if a particular stock is undervalued or overvalued. If you are able to perform the fundamental analysis perfectly, then you will also be able to point out investment opportunities that others have not yet noticed.

Some of the components of a stock that are analyzed are as follows, competitor analysis, external politics, trade agreements, news releases, global industry, political conditions within the country, press releases of the company, and financial statements of the company.

If there is a bad impact on any of these fundamental indicators, then there is a possibility that the share price will be negatively affected. Similarly, if there is a positive change in the indicators, the stock price of that particular company will be boosted.

How to Get Started with Technical Analysis?

If you are just a beginner, then here are some of the basic steps that you should implement in order to get started with technical analysis.

- **Develop a trading system:** This is the first step, and it means you have to identify a technical analysis strategy that works for you. For example, if you are a beginner, then you might go for the moving average crossover strategy. In this method, you will be keeping track of the two moving averages on any particular stock's changes in price.

- **Find the right strategy for your tradable security:** Not every strategy is meant for all securities. If your tradable securities are options, then you have to find the strategy that fits them. Sometimes, the parameter choices also start changing with the security you choose.

- **Choose the right brokerage account:** The next step is to choose the right brokerage account where you will be able to trade the type of security you have chosen. Not every brokerage account gives you the tools needed to perform technical analysis of options. The brokerage account you choose should have proper monitoring and tracking functionality with the technical indicators you need. Also, you need to make sure that your costs are low so that your profits are not affected.

- **Choose an interface to monitor trades:** Depending on the strategy you have chosen, the functionality you also need changes. So, choose your interface carefully.

- **See whether you need any more applications:** Sometimes, in order to maximize the performance, you might need other applications too. Some traders prefer trading on the go, and so they look for platforms that would give them mobile alerts. So, if there are any such special requirements, think about whether you need any more applications to support you.

Now, technical analysis for options trading is slightly different mainly because there is the subject of time decay in options. You cannot hold a position for an indefinite period of time. There is an expiration date for every option before which you will have to leave it. So, some of the common technical indicators that are used in this case have been discussed in the next section.

How to Get Started with Fundamental Analysis?

If you're anything like me, when you hear the word "fundamental analysis," you probably think about old men in suits with well-groomed beards and political ties. You may even make a reference to Gordon Gecko! Fundamental analysis isn't just for rich guys, but it's an essential part of any successful trading strategy.

Here, I'll show you how to get started with fundamental analysis using some pretty simple steps:

1. Identify the market's trend.

It is important to determine whether the market is trending up or down before you begin your fundamental analysis. This is called trend identification.

Forex traders generally use several tools to determine the market's trend, such as:

- Simple moving averages (SMA) and exponential moving averages (EMA).

- Retracement levels and trend lines. Channels and triangles.

- Stochastic oscillators.

- High-low-close trading range indices.

When you attach a specific time frame to each of these charts, you'll have a more precise view of the market's trends; you can also figure out how much profit or loss your trading plan might create over an extended period of time with each of them.

2. Determine which technical indicators are most relevant to the market's trend.

For this, you'll need to practice more and more.

3. Calculate a risk.

You probably know the basic risk-reward principle (i.e., "buy low, sell high"). However, you should also be aware that the ratio between price and underlying value is not always close to 1:1.

For example, if a stock that's trading at $30 per share, you can expect it to return about 3 percent of your investment per year ($30 * 8% = $3 per year), but the stock could lose 10 percent of its value in one year ($30 * 10% = $3). In this case, you can gain much more than you lose from the investment if the risk is small.

The same idea applies to Forex pairs: If the price moves in a range of 0.1-0.2 pips, it's not a big deal; however, when price moves in a range of 1-3 pips, it will create a lot of noise in the spread (i.e., the difference between the bid and ask). And when price moves into large ranges (5 pips or more), demand will be much higher than supply, resulting in a market imbalance that could result in slippage and potential losses.

4. Calculate a margin requirement for your position.

To calculate a possible loss, you need to figure out the maximum loss that your position will bring. You can do this by using logarithmic calculations.

For example, if you're trading a stock that's worth $100, and the market price moved up 0.2 pips today, then the stock is now worth $102; in this case, your margin requirement will be $1 for every penny movement, no more no less.

5. Calculate an initial stop loss for each pair and set it on your chart.

A "Stop" order is a command that tells your broker not to trade when a specific price has been reached.

You can use several types of stop-loss orders, but the most popular are:

- Stop-limit orders.

- Stop-loss orders.

- Stop-loss in points.

6. Calculate the exposure and risk capital before you enter a trade.

Some traders refer to this as an initial margin requirement or "margin." The professional forex brokers require your accounts to maintain a certain level of exposure in order to prevent any possible losses from running into your account's equity (e.g., the money you deposited into your account). Once again, it is very important that you make sure your margin requirement is greater than any possible loss that could run through the account and into negative territory.

7. Determine when you will sell your position.

This is easy, after you make some profit, of course!

8. Calculate the possible loss for each position you are in.

One of the best ways to analyze market risk is through a spreadsheet, which you can create with Microsoft Excel or Google Spreadsheets. Also, you can use an online forex calculator to calculate margin requirements and stop- losses without a spreadsheet: Forex Risk Calculator.

9. Decide whether or not your analysis makes sense for your trading plan, and adjust it accordingly.

Once again, I recommend that you start off with a simpler analysis, then proceed to a more complex analysis as your skills improve.

If you find it difficult to analyze the strength and weakness of a pair, simply compare the present value of the Forex pair to price movement over a specified period of time. This is called "momentum."

Advantages & Disadvantages

For Fundamental Analysis:

Advantages:

- Only sound financial data are used to perform fundamental analysis. Thus, there is no scope of personal bias anywhere.

- You will arrive at a proper recommendation to either buy or sell by using analytical and statistical tools.

- Several long-term trends of demographic, economic, consumer, and technological origin are considered.

- Rigorous financial analysis and accounting pave the way for understanding everything in-depth and leaves room for no mistakes.

Disadvantages:

- When you are considering the financials, some assumptions have to be made. So, I always advise everyone to consider both the worst and best scenarios. There can be unexpected legislative or economic changes at any time.

- The entire process of industry analysis takes up a lot of time, and it is definitely not a cakewalk.

For Technical Analysis:

Advantages:

- You come to know the possible entry and exit points in the trade. You get to know how the overall market is performing, and you can judge the overall sentiments that are running.

- When you notice patterns, you can predict directions of movement.

Disadvantages:

- The underlying fundamentals are not taken into consideration while performing technical analysis. And thus, several risks can crop up because of this.

- Sometimes, if your chart is full of too many indicators, then the signals can be confusing.

2

MONEY MANAGEMENT CONCEPT

Money Concept in Option Trading

When working with options, it can provide you with some good leveraging power. A trader will be able to buy an option position that will imitate their stock position quite a bit, but it will end up saving them a lot of money in the process.

Let's say that you saw that there was an opportunity to make a profitable trade, you were only able to spare about $1000 to purchase the stock, but you didn't know what options were available. If we were still talking about the cows from before, you would not be able to purchase even one cow for the money (remember that they are about $2,000 each without the options contract), and so you would completely miss out on the possibility to make a profit.

But, if you decided to purchase with an options contract, rather than purchasing the underlying asset outright, the dynamics have completely changed. This could result in an investment of just $250 to get started. The premium on the options contract is a fraction of the total cost, allowing you to get in on the trade for a lot less money. If you look into options contracts, you will be able to make more purchases, and potentially more money, compared to some of the other stock choices you can make.

Exercise and Expiration

When there's a lot of time left for the options contract to expire, chances are high that the price of the underlying asset will undergo significant changes. Thus, the premium will be high. On the other hand, as the expiration approaches, the chances of significant change in the price of underlying assets tend to diminish, thus lowering the premium. The date of expiration causes options to have a definitive nature. Thus, if the price of an option seems unbearable, you might consider waiting for the expiration date to thin out.

Delivery and Settlement

Every contract for options will have a strike price associated with it. Of any of the given index or stock that is traded, there are going to be various options contracts that correspond with various strike prices. These prices are determined ahead of time by the stock exchange where the stock is traded.

Analysis of Costs and Benefits in the Options

The leveraging power of options is great. Thus, a trader may acquire an option position similar to a stock position, but at a significantly lower price. With options trading, it is possible to make great profits without necessarily having large amounts of money. Individuals that operate on a tight budget have found options trading very accommodating. A shrewd trader can employ leverage to increase their trading power without necessarily injecting more capital.

Let's suppose that you had $1000 and wanted to invest in a company whose stock was trading at $20 per share. On the one hand, you could choose to buy the company's stocks and thus acquire 50 shares. If the stock price increases to $25, you would make a $5 profit for every share you own, and your total profit would be $250. This is a 25% return on investment! On the other hand, you could purchase call options on the same stock and gain the right to purchase it. Assuming that the call options with a $20 strike price were trading at $2, you could purchase 500 options, which would enable you to purchase 500 shares. Assuming that the stock price increased to $25, you could exercise your option to purchase 500 shares and, upon selling your shares, you'd make a grand total of $2500. This is a staggering 150% return on investment! The greatest appeal of options trading is that it enables traders to execute cost-efficient trades even as it widens their earning capacity.

Risks Leverage

We rarely talk about how we can troubleshoot arising problems, or even reduce the degree of financial risks we must take in the first place. Though by no means extensive, I've included a short (but hopefully helpful) preview of the ways in which we can work on doing this with the first 48 hours of trading.

- **Trade with this approach in mind**: focus your attention and effort toward avoiding risks, rather than securing potential rewards. If you're not convinced, think about this little statistic recorded from a 2013 U.S Trust survey: 60% of millionaire investors place more emphasis on avoiding unnecessary risks than securing potential capital gain.

- **Diversify your account**. This is essentially just a fancy word for "split up your money to make it safer." When you don't put all of your eggs in one basket, so to speak, you significantly (and technically eliminate) the risk of losing all of your money when one investment opportunity cracks or crumbles.

- **Keep a broker or brokerage close by**. Beginner traders can benefit greatly from having a highly-trained, experienced financial expert or professional just a phone call or drive away. When trades don't go your way, or you're simply not deriving the benefits you expected from trades, even within that initial 48-hour timeframe, a broker can assist and advise you on how to produce better results and generate more meaningful profit. Or they can attempt to remedy current, negative financial situations or trades.

Trading Rules You Should Know

The most common form of underlying assets that the majority of options contracts are based on are the shares of a publicly listed company. But an underlying asset can take other varied forms, such as the following:

- **Index options:** These have a close similarity to stock options, except that the index, not the shares, is what the options are based on.

- **Forex/Currency options:** The contracts of this nature give the owner the authority to purchase or sell off a certain currency at an agreed exchange rate.

- **Futures options:** The specified futures contract is the underlying security. A futures option allows the owner to enter into a specific futures contract.

- **Basket options:** The underlying asset can comprise a set of securities, such as currencies, stocks, commodities, and other financial securities.

- **Commodity options:** For this kind of contract, the underlying asset can be a commodity that is physical or based on futures contract.

3
OPTION STRATEGIES

Time to explore some option trading strategies. We will go from the easy to understand to the more complex. All are beginner-friendly, which means there many more option strategies you can learn out there once you become experienced.

Naked Call and Naked Puts

While naked calls and puts aren't regarded as complex trading strategies, they are interesting, risky ways of making money using options. Both strategies try to make money from the premiums alone but without an underlying asset to meet the promise they are making to the other trader. Trading platforms and brokers either require you to have money to cover your promise or be trustworthy. That trustworthiness is established by themselves. Each platform or broker will have its policies on how they implement this.

A naked call is when you sell a call option while you don't own the underlying financial assets. The fact that you have the option of selling your stock is crucial. It protects you from losses that are theoretically infinite.

Imagine Microsoft stock trading at $250. You believe the stock will go down, so you sell a call option with a strike price of $260 at a premium of $10. Microsoft's stock has to rise to about $270 to be profitable for the person who bought the call option from you.

If the Microsoft stock suddenly skyrockets, to say $500, the call buyer will exercise their option, meaning they will want to buy 100 Microsoft shares from you at $260 per share. But you don't have those shares. To fulfill that order, you will have to buy 100 Microsoft shares at $500 a share and then sell them to the call buyer at $260 a share. It means you have lost a total of $14,000 ($24,000 minus the premium).

Now, imagine the same scenario, but this time, you own 100 Microsoft shares. In other words, you have covered your call. You would miss out on the market rally, but at least you would have made $27,000 from the trade instead of losing money. The naked in the name is descriptive. This type of position exposes you to potentially unlimited risks. You might find yourself having to borrow money to close your position.

A naked put is when you sell a put option without having the funds or a short position to meet your side of the agreement if the put option is exercised. You need to show you have the means to cover your naked put to use one. Let's return to our Microsoft example to see how naked puts play out.

Microsoft is trading at $250. You sell a put option with a strike price of $200 with a premium of $20. The maximum profit you can make is from the premium, which is $2,000. The maximum you can lose is $20,000 ($200 x 100). Say Microsoft stock plummets by $100. The price of the stock is now $150. The put buyer will exercise their put option, meaning you will have to buy 100 shares at $200 a share. It costs you $20,000. If you want, you can hold on to the stock and see if it goes up again. When it rises, you can sell the stock and make your money again. But say the future of Microsoft stock isn't looking too well. You will find yourself having to sell it at $150 a share, receiving $15,000. You have lost $3,000 ($5,000 minus the premium).

A naked put gets worse and worse as the price of the underlying asset plummets. In the case that Microsoft goes bankrupt, its stock would be worth $0. But you would have to buy all the shares at $200, paying $20,000 and being left with $2,000 from the premium in your account. Although companies go bankrupt like this, it does not happen often. You should be aware of this possibility.

Naked options make a profit when they expire worthlessly.

Buy-Write Strategy

In this strategy, you buy a stock and then write a call option for it in a way that still leads you to profit when the call option gets exercised. Here's the bull call strategy in action.

Suppose you buy 100 shares of Ford, and you want to keep them. At the same time, you don't want to make extra money from the stock. Writing buy-write call options would be a good option for this because the likelihood of you losing the stock is low, and even when you do lose your stock, you have made a profit on it.

If Ford's share price is now $300, you will write a call option with a strike price of $340. Then you sell the call option for a premium of $30. If the stock hits $380, the person who bought the call option will exercise it because it is now profitable. You will sell them your stock at $340 per share plus the premium, meaning you would get $370 per share. It is still very high. You are only missing out on $10 per share. You still managed to sell your stock at a higher price than the one you got it at and very close to the going price.

Bull Call Strategy

A bull call strategy is when a trader uses two call options on the same underlying asset to reduce the cost of premium paid (Gentle, 2020). In this case, you buy a call option of Ford, then sell another call option on Ford. You would use the premium you received on the call option you sold to reduce the premium you have paid for the call option you have bought. Again, it seems better.

Say you see a Ford's call option with the premium of $30 and strike price of $100. It would mean you need the stock price to rise above $130 for the call option to start becoming profitable. However, you are not willing to spend $30 on the risk, so, you write a second call option on the Ford stock with a strike price of $125. You charge a $15 premium on it. You will receive a $15 premium from the call option you sold and use that with the money from your pocket to pay for the call option with a strike price of $100 and a premium of $30. So, you would be only spending $15 of your own money to finance the call option. You have halved the price of the premium!

Suppose the stock price reaches $135. You would exercise your call option. You can buy 100 shares at a strike rate of $100 plus the premium ($30 - $15 = $15). Meaning you would spend $11500 on it. If you sell them, you will make a profit of $2,000.

So what happens if the price is high enough for the person you sold the call option to make a profit? The stock price has to rise above $140 for it to be profitable for them. If it reaches $142, for example, they may decide to exercise their call and buy the stock from you at $12,500. That is the worst that can happen, but it also means you cannot make a profit from selling your stock at that price because the person you sold the call option will exercise their call, meaning you have to sell to them. So, your profit range is limited between buying and selling at $135 to $140. You cannot profit on price movements beyond that.

The advantage is that if the price does not rise that high, you would have spent 50% of the premium to earn profit.

Married Put

Married puts, as the name suggests are for investors who are in it for life—or as much as we can call life in the financial markets. It is for investors who are married to their stock. They have invested in a company for a long time, they like the benefits they get, and they don't want to lose their profit on the stock (Gentle, 2020).

Imagine you owned Ford stock when the price was still $10, and the company kept growing and improving. Its stock price rose exponentially to $150. You have made a lot of money. Then you begin to hear stories of a competitor possibly surpassing the company and taking their most profitable market. You are worried that this may be bad news for your stock. Your stock may fall to about $50 per share if the company does not handle itself well. You execute a married put to protect your wealth.

A married put is when an investor buys an option of their stock that is at the money or close. So, you would buy a put option of your 100 Ford shares for a premium of $30 per share at a strike price of $148, for instance. Say your worst fears come true, and the stock plummets to $50 per share. You have an option to exercise your put option and sell your shares for 148 per share. Minus the premium, you would pocket $118 per share. That is over 50% of the going price of the shares. If you decide to buy the shares again, you would have made a profit of $68 per share. It's a lot of money.

Married puts are mainly about recovering from a loss or using puts as insurance. Say your worst fear doesn't come true, and Ford blows the competition out the water, and your stock price rises to $220 per share. That is a massive win. You only spent $30 per share to protect your wealth. That's nothing compared to what you have gained. Married puts also allow traders to stay in position longer to see if their stock recovers or rallies past the strike price. It is a responsible thing to do. You don't want to jump out of a stock from panic only to hear of the stock rising past the value you sold it at.

Bear Call Spread Strategy

As the name suggests, this is a bearish strategy, meaning it is entered on the assumption that the price of the underlying asset will go down. A bear call spread is when you write a call option with a high premium and buy a low premium call option on the same underlying asset (Gentle, 2020). When you do this, you will collect the premium, which becomes your credit and profit. The call option you bought is to protect you from losing all the money you made from the premium. The bought call option can function to breakeven.

Imagine you have $10,000 in your trading account, and you want to execute a bear call spread. You spot a stock going at $100 a share. From your analysis, it is pretty clear that the stock is going to continue to go down. So, wouldn't it be great if you wrote a call option on this stock so that you can collect premiums from bullish traders? It would. So you write a call option with a strike price of $100 with a premium of $20. The stock will have to rise above the $120 mark to start making a profit for the buyer. When someone buys the option, that is $2,000 in your account.

I am sure you realize if the price of the stock rose to $135, you would have to buy 100 shares. This would cost you $13,500. At this point, you would now owe $3,500. The person you sold the call option to now buys the stock from you at $105 a share. Meaning your new balance will be $6,500. That is down by $3,500 from the $10,000 you had in the beginning. So, this was a stupid gamble. You can protect yourself from losses by buying a call option.

Here's what happens when we factor in the second call option you bought at a strike rate of $105. Let's say the call option costs you $10 a share. When the person you sold a call option to exercise their call option. You exercise yours, avoiding paying $135 per share and paying $105 a share and then selling those shares at $100 a share to the person you sold the high premium call option to.

Here's the math. You wrote a call option, and you got $2,000 in your account, making the total $12,000. Then you spent $1,000 to buy a call option. Your balance is now $11,000. Then the call buyer exercises their call option because it has reached profitability. To fulfill their order, you exercise your call option by buying 100 shares below market at $105 a share. This costs you $10,500. Your balance is now $500. You then sell those shares to the call buyer at $100 a share, meaning you end up with a total of $10,500 in your account. That is up from $10,000. If both options expire without being profitable, you would still have made a $1,000 profit from the premium alone ($2,000–$1,000).

As you may have noticed, the bear call spread strategy caps your profit and losses. The maximum you can make is what you get from premiums. And the maximum you can lose on a trade is the difference between the options' strike prices.

Bull Put Spread Strategy

The bull put is a bullish strategy. Think of it as the sister of the bear call spread strategy. It is the same strategy, but it involves two put options. In this instance, the maximum you can make from a trade is the premium paid. Let's turn to an example.

Imagine you have $10,000 in your trading account. You look at Y stock that is trading at $100 a share. You believe the stock will go up, so you sell a put option with a strike price of $105 for $15. The person who buys the put option from you believes Y stock will fall. Remember that put option buyers make a profit by shorting the stock. When they buy the option from you, your new account balance is $11,500. Then you buy a put option for Y stock at a $95 strike price for $3. That is going to cost you $300, so you are now left with $11,200. $1,200 is the maximum profit you can make from this trade. If the stock remains above $90 until the expiry date, you are in the clear.

However, let's say the stock falls to $85, for example. The option buyer will sell their Y shares to you at $105 a share. That will cost you $10,500, meaning you will be left with $700 in your account. Then you would exercise your put option by selling those Y stock shares for $95 a share. You will make $9,500, meaning your new account balance will be $10,200. That is up by $200. The maximum profit you can make is the premium you get. To find that out, you need to subtract the premium paid from the premium received ($1500 - $300 = $1200)

The Straddle

All of our examples are based on a stock market that moves but isn't very volatile. That assumes some kind of predictability and reasonable guesses. For instance, we have talked about making bets based on a piece of news or an upcoming earnings report, but some markets are just too strange to predict reasonably enough. This does not mean that we cannot predict anything or calculate probability. We can. It means that it is very hard, usually because people act in unpredictable ways. In short, some markets are just too darn volatile.

Instead of trying to fight against it or to beat it, some traders are doing something a lot cooler: using that unpredictability to garner profits. That is where the straddle strategy was born. It's for those who seek to make money from unpredictability, possibly earning a lot more. So, how does it work?

Here's how it works. Say you own stock Y that is very unpredictable and keeps having strange movements. To make some money from this stock, you would buy a put option to profit from a sharp decline. Then you would buy a call option to profit from a sharp increase. If there is a sharp increase, you exercise your call option, and if there is a sharp decline, you exercise your put option. You will have to make sure that a transaction will give you profitability when all is factored in.

Currently, company Y stock is valued at $100 per share. You buy a put option with a strike price of $95 and a premium of $7. Then you can buy a call option that has a strike price of $105 and a premium of $7. You have spent $1,400 on premiums for both contracts. This means the price of the underlying asset has to move by more than $14 in either direction for you to start seeing any profit. What is amazing about the straddle is that you can benefit twice in one period.

Say the Y stock plummets to $80 a share. You can exercise your put option. Sell your Y stock for $95 and get $9,500. You can repurchase the stock at $80 a share. This will cost you $8,000, meaning you will have $1,500 leftover. Minus the premium you paid, your profit is $100. But you can significantly make more money depending on how sharply the price rises and falls. If Y shares' price was to rise to $120 a share, you would see the same profit margins.

Now, imagine the stock falls as we have predicted, and you are now sitting on $100 profit. Your call option hasn't expired yet. If the price of Y stock rises sharply, you can increase your profit. You will be able to profit as long as Y's price is above the strike price because you have already covered the cost of your premium by exercising your call option. So, if Y stock suddenly picks up from $80 a share and reaches $110 a share, you can exercise your call option to buy 100 shares at $105. Then, sell those shares at $110. You will make $500. Now your profit will total $600. You can also watch to see if the price goes any further above the strike price, yielding you more profit.

You can see why this strategy is called the straddle. You have covered two opposing positions to make the maximum profit. The most traders can lose in this position is the money they pay in premiums. The options writers are the ones who are at a greater risk of losing more than they bargained for.

A variation of the straddle is called the strangle. **Strangle strategy** shows a preference for one likelihood over the other. In our straddle example, the strike prices are equally further away from the current Y stock price. This means we regarded it as a 50/50 chance that the Y stock would rise and fall sharply. That is why we took equal risks.

The strangle strategy applies when we believe one outcome is a lot more likely than the other, but we still don't trust the stock. For instance, we might believe that Y stock might rise mildly but fall sharply. In that situation, how should we buy our put and call options for Y stock?

If we believe this, it means it is not worth paying a lot for the call option. So we would avoid buying call options in the money or at the money because that would be too expensive since we don't believe the stock will rise sharply. So we will purchase a call option further out of the money. We do this because it is cheaper, and it will be able to catch some profit if the Y stock shoots up sharply. Maybe we would spend $4 for a call option with a strike price of $114.

Because we believe the stock will fall sharply, it makes more sense to buy an in the money put option, even if that put option is expensive. The put option doesn't have to be in the money. Close enough counts, too. So we could see ourselves paying $10 for a call option with a strike price of $98. We still made the same investment of $1,400. If we are proven correct, what happens?

If the stock fell to $70 as we suspected, we would make a lot of money. We would sell stock at $98 a share and repurchase the stock at $70 a share, making a profit of $1,800 from the put alone. If you subtract our call investment, we will make a profit of $1,400. That is over 100% profit.

Here's the math. You made an initial investment of $1,400 (14 x 100) for both the call and put the option. When the stock fell, you sold your shares, receiving $9,800 (100 x 98) for them. Then you bought them back immediately for $7,000 (70 x 100), leaving you with $2,800 (9800- 7000). Subtracting your initial investment, $1,400, you are left with $1,400 as your profit.

The strangle pays you more if your bias for the call or the put option is proven right. This is why some people will often prefer it over the straddle and only use the straddle when they are absolutely not sure which direction the stock price will move, but they know it will.

Protective Collar

As the name suggests, this strategy is all about protecting your investment, but–get this–without paying for it. Traders use the protective collar when they have been long on a stock, and they believe the stock has hit a wall, and they want to close their position at a profit (Gentle, 2020).

You bought 1,000 shares of a startup when it was just $4 a share. It was $4,000. They continued to experience growth, and now they appear to be hitting a wall as competitors emerge and face some backlash over some of their practices. Today, the price of one share is $500. Meaning if you sold today, you could make $500,000. But selling thousands of shares can take a while, and by the time the order is fulfilled, the price might have dipped as more news continues to come out.

You don't think the stock price will increase. So you sell the call option at a strike price of $510 for the premium of $20 a share. There are people out there who would be willing to make that bet. So you write 10 options like these of your 1,000 shares. The premium you will get for all of them is $20,000.

Then you take that money and buy put options on the same shares that cost the same. These put options will likely be out of the money. You can buy a put option with a strike price of $480 for a $20 premium per share. See? You did not pay for this protection. You know, the price will fall, because of the news lately. If it doesn't fall, great! You spent none of your own money on the put option. If it rises, it probably won't rise by much. But if it does, you would have made a lot on your initial investment of $4,000. If the price falls below $480, you will be able to walk out with $480,000. That is a lot of money from $4,000.

The great thing about this strategy is that it is like insurance you don't pay for. You win whatever happens because your goal is all about preventing loss.

Iron Condor Strategy

The iron condor strategy is made up of four options: two puts and two calls. The aim of this strategy is to profit from premiums and minimize risk. It works best when all options expire worthless.

To execute an iron condor strategy, you will need to sell and buy call and put options. You would sell a call option close to the money and buy a call option out of the money. Then, you would sell a put option closer to the current stock price and buy one further away from the price. All this action is performed on the same underlying asset. The inner options have higher premiums, and the outer ones have lower premiums. Outer options function as a cap, and the inner ones extract profit. Also, the iron condor strategy can be configured with a bias that is bullish or bearish. It is all up to you.

Let's turn to an example. Say you have Microsoft stock trading at $200, and it is stable–low volatility. So you want to make money from the low volatility. You can do that using the iron condor strategy. You would sell a call option with a strike price of $210 at a premium of $15. You then buy a call option with a strike price of $220 and a premium of $5. Then you sell a put option with a strike price of $190 for a $15 premium. Then you buy a put option with a premium of $5 and a strike price of $185.

As soon as you open this position, you will receive $3,000 in premiums. Then you will spend $1,000 on buying your options, meaning you will get $2000 in your account. That money is your profit. If the options expire worthless, you will keep all your money. Seeing there is low volatility in the market, that is likely to happen.

In the unlikely event that Microsoft suddenly buys Alphabet and its stock price soars to $900 a share, the person who bought the call option from you will exercise their call option. When that happens, you will buy the

Microsoft stock at $220 and sell the stock at $210 to them. You cap your loss to $1,000, which means your profit halves. The second call protected you from losing close to $80,000. That is impressive.

In the case that Microsoft goes bankrupt, the person who bought the put option from you will sell their stock to you at $190 a share. It will cost you $19,000. Then you will exercise your put option, selling that stock for $185, receiving $18,500 in your account. In this instance, you only lost one-third of your profit. The second put has acted as protection.

When putting an iron condor, you need to pick a low volatility stock that will only go up or down if the worst happens (not both). Suppose the stock goes up and down during the month. You will have your profit reduced twice. In our example, it means you will only make a $500 profit. It would probably be less when you consider commissions and fees. Our example shows an iron condor strategy with a bearish bias. We have applied more protection in the put options than we have to the call option. For instance, the maximum you can lose if the stock goes up is $1,000, and the maximum you can lose if the stock plummets is $500.

Remember that all of these options share the same expiry date and underlying asset.

4

BASICS OF OPTION PRICING

Options traders need to comprehend extra factors that influence an option's price and the complexity of picking the right technique. When a stockbroker turns out to be acceptable at foreseeing the future price movement. the person may believe it is a simple change from options, but this isn't accurate. Options traders must deal with 3 shifting parameters that influence the price: the price of the underlying time, volatility, and security. Changes in any of these factors influence the option's value.

Option pricing hypothesis utilizes factors (exercise price, stock price, interest rate, time to expiration, volatility) to hypothetically value an option. It gives an estimation of an option's reasonable value which traders join into their techniques to maximize profits. Some ordinarily utilized models to value options are Black-Scholes, Monte-Carlo, and Binomial Option Pricing. These speculations have wide margins for error because of deriving their values from different assets, typically the cost of an organization's basic stock. There are scientific formulas intended to compute the fair reasonable value of an option. The broker simply inputs known factors and finds a solution that depicts what the option should be worth.

The essential objective of any option pricing model is to compute the probability that an option will be worked out, or be in-the-money (ITM), at lapse. Basic asset value (stock value), interest rate, exercise price, time to expiration, and volatility, which is the number of days between the computation date and the option's exercise date, are usually utilized variables that are input into logical models to derive an option's hypothetical fair value.

The Greeks

The concept behind delta is actually pretty straightforward and easy to apply. It tells you how much the price of an option is going to change if the price of the underlying stock changes by one dollar. Consider a delta of 0.68. If the underlying stock changes by one dollar, that tells us that the price of the option will change by $0.68.

The way the Delta changes with time depends on a few factors. Let's take an in-the-money call option first. When it is in the money, delta increases with the passage of time. The reason why this happens is that extrinsic value is decreasing, while intrinsic value remains directly proportional to the price of the stock. Therefore, delta will increase. At first, this effect is barely noticeable if at all. The less time remaining for the option, the more noticeable it will be.

Now let's consider a call option that is out of the money. In that case, Delta will decrease.

For comparison suppose that we have a call option with a strike price equal to $100. Suppose further that there are 10 days left to expiration. If the underlying stock price is $99 (so that the call option is out of the money) delta is 0.43. On the other hand, if the share price was $101, (so that the option was in the money), delta would be 0.59.

This demonstrates that when the option goes in the money, with all else being equal, it is more heavily influenced by the price of the underlying shares.

Under the conditions specified with the price of the stock at $101, the price of the call option is $2.54. Suppose that the price of the stock goes up to $102. Since Delta is 0.59, we expect the $1 rise in share price to raise the price of the option by $0.59, to $3.13.

It raises it a little more, to $3.16, so it was a pretty good estimate. As the price changes delta changes as well. In this case, it jumped to 0.66, meaning that an additional rise in price by $1 will have a greater impact.

Of course, that cuts both ways; delta gives us an estimate of how much the price of the option will drop as well. If we have a value of delta equal to 0.66, we expect a $2 drop in share price to lead to a drop in the price of the option by $1.32. What actually happens is that the price of the call drops down to $1.98, not quite as much as expected. A declining share price means a declining delta, and in this example, it drops to 0.51. This implies that the next dollar that the share price drops will have less impact.

When options are at the money, delta will be close to 0.50 in all cases.

For call options, delta is a positive value. It ranges from zero all the way to up to 1.0. The more that the option goes in the money, the higher that Delta will be.

Let's consider our share price at a hundred dollars and suppose instead that we were looking at an option with a strike price of $90. In that case, delta is a very strong 0.98. Therefore, we would expect the price of the option to rise by nearly $1 for every $1 rise in share price. The price of this option under these conditions will be $10.04. Now, if we increase the share price by $1, we find that the price of the option will increase to $11.02. So, the correspondence between the actual change in option price and delta gets stronger, the more "in the money" the option is. Continuing our current example, a strike price of $85 would give us a call option with a delta of exactly 1.0.

If an option is out of money, the closer it gets to expiration the smaller delta gets. In fact, it will quickly go to zero.

Now let's have a look at put options.

For put options, delta is given as a negative value. So, the range for a put option is from zero to -1.0. The meaning is basically the same. It is a negative value because, in the case of put options, price movements of puts move in the opposite direction to stock value. In other words, put options become more valuable as stock prices drop.

The negative sign indicates that a drop in the price of a share of stock by a dollar is going to cause a rise in the option price—when we are talking about put options.

This means that changes in share price are going to be a little more influential for the option. If a put option is strongly in the money, delta will approach -1.0. Remember that, as the expiration date approaches for a call option, delta goes to zero if the option is out of the money. Put options exhibit the same behavior.

Delta can also be thought of in different ways. For example, it can estimate the probability that an option will expire in the money. So, let's say that you have a call option with the Delta of 0.7. That tells you that there is a 70% chance that the option will expire in the money. Another call option, that had a delta of 0.5, only has a 50% chance of expiring in the money. But remember that delta is dynamic, so that value is only the probability at this very moment. A significant change in stock price might change the situation, and one more business day will also impact it.

Gamma

Now, let's have a look at the next Greek, which is Gamma. This one is a little bit more obscure. Gamma can be thought of as the second derivative if you have experience with calculus. If you have no experience with calculus or you want to forget it, I apologize for the headache.

Basically, what that means is that Gamma gives the rate at which delta will change if there is a one-dollar change in the underlying stock price. As a side note, if you do remember from calculus, a derivative of position with time is speed or velocity. So, you can think of Delta as giving the speed or velocity in the change of price of the option.

Gamma, in this analogy, would be the acceleration in the change of the option price. Understanding the details and all the mathematics is not important for most options traders. However, you can keep some basic rules of thumb in mind. The key point is this. The higher gamma is the more responsive to changes the option is going to be in the underlying stock price.

Another way to think of this is to know that Delta changes every time the underlying stock price changes. So, Delta is only as good as the value that we see at a given instance. You can use Gamma to estimate how Delta will change when there is price movement. The further you are from expiration, the higher the Gamma will be.

The more an option goes in the money, the smaller Gamma will get. What that means is that Delta won't be changing as much for a given change in the price of the underlying stock if the option is in the money. If Delta goes to 1.0, then Gamma will go to zero.

Theta

It is a fact that the extrinsic value of an option is going to decrease as time passes. There is simply no way around this. When an option is further away from the expiration date, there are more opportunities for the stock price to fluctuate. This means that fluctuations in the stock price over a longer period of time could put an option that is currently out of the money, in the money. As you get closer to expiration, there are simply fewer opportunities for that to happen. So, an out-of-the-money option is not going to have as much value as days pass.

If you just play around with options prices using a calculator or watch them on the markets, it might seem a little bit mysterious how the extrinsic value changes. But you can use Theta to get an idea of what is happening. Theta gives an estimate of how much the price of the option will decrease each passing day. Specifically, it tells you how much the extrinsic or time value of the option will decrease.

Since Theta is telling you how much the extrinsic value is going to decrease, it is listed as a negative number. Consider an option with a $50 strike price and a share price of $53. At 15 days to expiration, Theta is -0.027 for a call option, and -0.026 for a put option. Let's look at the call option; the principle is about the same for both. This tells us that the extrinsic value at 14 days will drop by about $0.03. At 15 days to expiration, the extrinsic value is $0.29 for the call option. So, we are going to expect it to drop to $0.26 the following day. As a matter of fact, this is exactly what happens.

Time decay is exponential and not linear. If an option is in the money, Theta will decrease in value as the expiration date approaches. If it is out of the money, then it will increase. This indicates that an out-of-the-money option is going to lose value faster, the closer you get the expiration date.

An in-the-money option will smoothly lose extrinsic value as the expiration date approaches. At-the-money options will gain in value as the expiration date approaches. For at-the-money options, extrinsic value represents a higher proportion of their price as compared to other options. Even though Theta will be smaller for out-of-the-money options, it still represents agreater percentage of losses in price, because extrinsic value represents 100% of the total worth.

In any case, options always lose extrinsic value as the expiration date approaches.

5

STRANGLES AND STRADDLES

Strangles and Straddles are the two options techniques that permit an investor to profit by critical moves in a stock's price, whether the stock goes up or down. The two methodologies comprise of purchasing an equal number of put and call options with the same termination date. The difference is that the strangle has two diverse strike prices, while the straddle has a typical strike price.

Options are a type of subsidiary security, which means the cost of the options is intrinsically connected to the cost of something different. If you purchase an options contract, you have the right, however not the responsibility to purchase or sell an underlying asset at a set cost before a particular date.

A call option gives an investor the option to purchase stock, and a put option gives an investor the option to sell a stock. The strike price of an option contract is the cost at which an underlying stock can be purchased or sold. The stock must transcend this price for calls or fall underneath for puts before a position can be practiced for a profit.

KEY TAKEAWAYS

- Strangles and Straddles are options techniques investors use to profit by huge moves in a stock's value, paying little regard to the direction.

- Straddles are helpful when it's unclear what direction the stock price may move in, with the goal that way the investor is secured, paying little regard to the result.

- Strangles are valuable when the financial specialist believes it's likely that the stock will move one way or the other however needs to be protected in the event of some unforeseen circumstance.

- Investors ought to become familiar with the perplexing tax laws around how to account for options trading profit and losses.

Straddle

The straddle trade is one path for a broker to benefit from the price movement of an underlying asset. Suppose an organization is scheduled to discharge its most recent income results about three weeks, however, you have no clue whether the news will be positive or negative. These weeks before the news discharge would be a decent time to go into a straddle since when the outcomes are discharged, the stock is probably going to move sharply lower or higher.

How about we assume that the stock is trading at $15 in the period of April. Assume a $15 call option for June has a cost of $2, while the cost of the $15 put option for June is $1. A straddle is accomplished by purchasing both the put and the call for an aggregate of $300: ($2 + $1) x 100 shares for each option contract = $300.

The straddle will increment in price if the stock moves higher (due to the long call option) or if the stock goes lower (due to the long put option). Profits will be gotten as long as the price of the stock moves by more than $3 per share in either course.

Strangle

Another way to manage options is the strangle position. While a straddle has no directional inclination, a strangle is utilized when the financial specialist accepts the stock has a superior possibility of moving a specific direction, however, it might still like to be secured on account of a negative move.

For instance, suppose you believe an organization's outcomes will be positive, which means you require less downside protection. Rather than purchasing the put option with the strike price of $15 for $1, possibly you take a look at purchasing the $12.50 strike that has a cost of $0.25. This trade would cost less than the straddle and require less of an upward move for you to equal the initial investment (or break- even).

Utilizing the lower-strike put option in this strangle will still secure you against the outrageous downside, while likewise placing you in a superior position to pick up from a positive declaration.

These techniques consolidate put and call options to make positions where a speculator can benefit from price swings in the underlying stock, even when the financial specialist doesn't know what direction the price will swing.

In the straddle technique, a financial specialist or an investor holds a position in a put or call option with the same strike price and lapse dates for the same underlying stock. In the strangle technique, a speculator/investor holds a put and call option with the same termination dates however unique strike prices for the same underlying stock.

In a straddle position, an investor holds a put and call option that is "at-the-money." In a strangle position, a speculator/investor holds a put and call option that is "out-of-the-money." Due to this, getting into a strangle position is commonly less expensive than getting into a straddle position.

In the wake of taking a look at these two models, investors should understand how the straddle and strangle options work. These techniques are effective tools that can be utilized when an investor wants to profit from an unpredictable or volatile stock.

6

IRON CONDOR AND BUTTERFLY

What Is an Iron Condor?

An iron condor is an options technique made with four options comprising of two puts (one short and one long) and two calls (one short and one long), and four strike prices, all with the same termination date. The objective is to profit from low unpredictability in the underlying asset. At the end of the day, the iron condor procures the most extreme profit when the underlying asset closes between the center strike prices at expiration.

The iron condor has a comparative result as a normal condor spread, however, it utilizes both puts and calls rather than just calls or just puts. Both the condor and the iron condor are expansions of the iron butterfly and butterfly spread, respectively.

KEY TAKEAWAYS

- An iron condor is ordinarily an unbiased technique and profits the most when the underlying asset does not move a lot. Although, the technique can be developed with a bearish or bullish bias.

- The iron condor is made out of four options: a purchased put further OTM and a sold put nearer to the money, and a purchased call further OTM and a sold call nearer to the money.

- Profit is topped at the premium gotten while the risk is likewise topped at the contrast between the purchased and sold call strikes and the purchased and sold put strikes (less the premium got).

Understanding the Iron Condor

The technique has constrained upside and downside risk due to the low and high strike options, the wings, secure against noteworthy moves in either direction. Due to this constrained risk, its profit potential is likewise restricted. The commission can be an eminent factor here, as there are four options involved.

For this technique, the dealer in a perfect world might like all of the options to worthlessly expire, which is just conceivable if the underlying asset closes between the middle two-strike costs at termination. There will probably be an expense to close the trade if it is successful. If it isn't, the loss is still constrained.

One approach to think about an iron condor is having a long strangle within a bigger, short strangle (or the other way around).

<u>The development of the strategy is as follows:</u>

1. Buy one out of the money (OTM) put with a strike cost beneath the present cost of the underlying asset. The out of the money put option will secure against a huge downside move to the underlying asset.

2. Sell one OTM or at the money (ATM) put with a strike value nearer to the present cost of the underlying asset.

3. Sell one OTM or ATM call with a strike cost over the present cost of the underlying asset.

4. Buy one OTM call with a strike cost further over the present cost of the underlying asset. The out of the money call option will secure against a considerable upside move.

The options that are additionally out of money, known as the wings, are both long positions. Since both of these options are farther from the money, their premiums are lower than the two composed options, so there is a net credit to the record while placing the trade.

By choosing distinctive strike prices, it is conceivable to make the technique lean bearish or bullish. For instance, if both the center strike prices are over the present cost of the underlying asset, the dealer seeks after a little ascent in its cost by expiration. It still has limited risk and limited reward.

Iron Condor Losses and Profits

The most extreme profits for an iron condor is the amount of credit, or premium, gotten for making the four-leg options position.

The most extreme loss is likewise topped. The greatest loss is the contrast between the short call and long call strikes, or the short put and long put strikes. Lessen the shortfall by the net credits gotten, however, then add commissions to get the absolute loss for the trade.

The greatest loss occurs if the value moves over the long call strike (which is higher than the sold call strike) or underneath the long-put strike (which is lower than the sold put strike).

Case of an Iron Condor on a Stock

Let's assume that an investor believes that Apple Inc. will be generally level in terms of price over the following two months. They choose to actualize an iron condor. The stock is presently trading at $212.26.

They sell a call with a $215 strike, which gives them $7.63 in premium. They purchase a call with a strike of $220, which costs them $5.35. The credit on these 2 legs is $2.28, or $228 for one contract. The trade is just half complete, however.

Also, the broker sells a put with a strike of $210, which results in a premium gotten of $7.20. They additionally purchase a put with a strike of $205, costing $5.52. The net credit on these 2 legs is $1.68 or $168 if trading one contract on each.

The entire credit for the position is $3.96 ($2.28 + $1.68), or $396. This is the greatest profit the broker can make. This greatest profit occurs if all the options terminate worthless, which implies the cost must be somewhere in the range of $215 and $210 when termination occurs in two months. If the price is above $215 or beneath $210, the dealer could still make a diminished profit, however, it could likewise lose money.

The loss gets bigger if the price of Apple stock methodologies the upper call strike ($220) or the lower put strike ($205). The most extreme loss occurs if the cost of the stock trades above $220 or beneath $205.

Assume the stock at termination is $225. This is over the upper call strike value, which implies the broker is facing the most extreme conceivable loss. The sold call is losing $10 ($225 - $215) while the purchased call is making $5 ($225 - $220). The puts expire. The broker/trade loses $5, or $500 total, but they additionally got $396 in premiums. In this manner, the loss is topped at $104 in addition to commissions.

Let's assume the cost of Apple rather dropped, but not beneath the lower put threshold. It decreases to $208. The short call is losing $2 ($208 - $210), or $200, while the long put lapses useless. The calls additionally expire. The dealer loses $200 on the position, however, he got $396 in premium credits. In this way, they still make $196, fewer commission costs.

IRON BUTTERFLY

What is an Iron Butterfly?

An iron butterfly is an options trade that utilizes four distinct contracts as a feature of a technique to benefit from futures price or stocks that move within a characterized range. The trade is likewise developed to profit by a decrease in implied volatility. The way to utilizing this trade as a feature of an effective trading technique is conjecture when option costs are probably going to decrease in value generally. This normally happens during periods of a mild upward trend or sideways movement. The trade is also called "Iron Fly."

KEY TAKEAWAYS

- Iron Butterfly trades are utilized as an approach to benefit from price movement in a thin range during a time of reducing implied volatility.

- The development of the trade is like that of a short-straddle trade with a long put and long call option bought for protection.

- Traders should be aware of commissions to be certain they can utilize this strategy successfully in their accounts.

- Traders should know that his trade could prompt a broker to procure the stock after expiration.

How an Iron Butterfly Works

The Iron Butterfly trade is made with four options comprising of two put options and two call options. These puts and calls are spread out more than three strike prices, all with the same termination date. The objective is to profit from conditions where the value remains genuinely steady and the options exhibit declining historical and implied volatility.

It can likewise be thought of as a consolidated option trade utilizing both a long strangle and a short straddle, with the strangle positioned on two additional strikes below and above the middle strike price and the straddle positioned on the middle of the three-strikes price.

The trade receives the maximum profit when the underlying assets close precisely on the center strike price at the end of termination. A broker will build an Iron Butterfly trade with the following advances.

1. The broker initially distinguishes a price at which they forecast the underlying asset will lay on a given day later. This is the objective price.

2. The broker will utilize options that expire that day or close to that day they forecast the objective cost.

3. The broker gets one call option with a strike value well over the objective price. This call option is required to be out-of-the-money at the hour of expiration. It will secure against a critical upward move in the underlying asset and top any potential loss at a defined sum should the exchange/trade not go as forecast.

4. The broker sells both a put and a call option utilizing the strike cost nearest the objective cost or objective price. This strike price will be lower than the call option bought in the past step and higher than the put option in the subsequent step.

5. The broker gets one put option with a strike value well beneath the objective cost. This put option is required to be out-of-the-money at the hour of termination. It will protect against a significant descending move in the underlying asset and top any

potential loss at a characterized sum should the trade not go as forecast.

The strike prices for the option contracts sold in steps three and two ought to be far enough apart to account for a scope of development in the underlying. This will permit the dealer to have the option to forecast the scope of effective value development instead of a thin range close to the objective price.

For instance, if the dealer feels that, throughout the following fourteen days, the underlying could land at the cost of $50, and be within a range of $5 higher or $5 lower from that target value, then the trader should sell a put and a call option with a strike price of $50 and should buy a call option at least $5 higher, and a put option at least $5 lower, than the $50 target cost. In principle, this makes a higher probability that the value action can land and stay in a beneficial range on or close to the day that the options expire.

Deconstructing the Iron Butterfly

The strategy has restricted the upside profit potential by structure. It is a credit-spread technique, implying that the dealer sells option premiums and takes credit for the price of the options at the beginning of the trade. The broker expects that the value of the options will lessen and culminate in an essentially lesser value, or no value at all. The broker in this manner plans to keep as much of the credit as could reasonably be expected.

The technique has characterized risk because of the low and high strike (the wings), protect against huge moves in either direction. It ought to be noticed that commission costs are constantly a factor with this technique since four options are involved. Traders will need to verify that the maximum potential profit isn't altogether dissolved by the commissions charged by their broker.

The Iron butterfly trade profits as lapse day draw near if the value lands within a range close to the middle strike price. The middle strike is where the merchant sells both a put option (a short strangle). The trade lessens in value as the price floats away from the middle strike, either lower or higher, and arrives at a point of maximum loss as the value moves either underneath the lower strike price or over the higher strike price.

CONCLUSION

I hope you have found this book helpful. Instead of spending our last moments going over what we learned, I think it would be better to talk about what your next steps should be.

The first thing you should do is to learn technical analysis and fundamental analysis. Technical analysis will help you read stocks, graphs, and other factors on the trading platform better, enabling you to make better decisions with your financial instruments. Fundamental analysis is about appraising the value of the stock themselves, away from market forces. Both are very powerful tools to have as a trade, so I would encourage learning them. You don't have to, but it will help a lot.

Secondly, find a trading community of beginners like you or start one. Lastly, don't stop learning. The day you stop learning is the day you stop growing.

All the best!

www.ingramcontent.com/pod-product-compliance
Lightning Source LLC
Chambersburg PA
CBHW071226130726
47998CB00002B/844